Welcome to the Kingdom, its taxonomies and subjugations, its streets and kick ass bards. There are many ways to read *La Chica's Field Guide*: a testament to the exponential speed of inequities; a chronicling of a third-generation Japanese American woman's kamikaze-like memory, witness, and resistance; an invocation of the epic power of the familial and the communal as evidenced by the simplest joys and our deepest sorrows. Amidst all of it, is the brilliant, resolute, invincible language of Jennifer Hasegawa. "Astounding alien / clean progenitor of the / new tongue of the ages. She / is here."

— Aja Couchois Duncan, author of *Restless Continent*, winner of the California Book Award

Jennifer Hasegawa's surreal, spectacular intelligence crackles through *La Chica's Field Guide to Banzai Living* like high-voltage current through a trunk line. Like its throw-down title, this book mixes the flirty with the elucidating and the go-for-broke. The section names—Propulsion Kingdom, Guidance Kingdom, Payload Kingdom—come from rocket technology, and in fact, outer space and aliens materialize in several poems. But technological displacement sits alongside grounded attention to life on earth. When Hasegawa takes on violent events—9/11, the Paris attacks—these overwhelming subjects yield to her human-scale scrutiny in epiphanies that let us feel again, even in the chaos—

The boom
flipped the room and bones

dropped from our pockets.

Many poems reveal Hasegawa's tender attachment to family in her native Hawai'i, to the sagas of daily life and natural beauty there, which bow but don't break under the ongoing pressures of colonization. This may be the key to Hasegawa's poetics: the resilience, the fierce intelligence, the banzai resolve to 'live for ten thousand years', not as a war cry but as a love letter, To Anyone Who Can't Get Home.

— Mary Burger, author of *Then Go On,*
A Partial Handbook for Navigators, and *Sonny*

Buckle up for Jennifer Hasegawa's exhilarating ride, whatever sort of displaced being you might be—from immigrant to extraterrestrial—and consult this manual. Follow the poems as they careen through assorted omens and "ghosts of sovereignty." Touching down in Hawai'i, California, and other parts of the world, Hasegawa carries her baggage with aplomb. She's all-too-aware of how old family folkways can linger with the "slow-burrowing hoodoo /of suggestion." And she's brazen enough to push through to the next realm of possibilities: "Our faces, // oh our glistening faces // will flex in recognition; / flash their alphabet of atoms, / to spell out a new world." Let her show you the turns—both thorny and tender—and you just might awaken there.

— Molly Bendall, author of *Watchful*

In the West, the word "banzai" was mostly recognized as the WWII battle cry of kamikaze pilots, but in truth, the word literally means 10,000 years and is associated with wishes for long life and celebration. It is a word that is both complex and compelling. The same could be said for the poems in Hasegawa's *La Chica's Field Guide to Banzai Living*. The collection takes us from Hawai'i to the U.S. Continent to Babylon to outer space, and Hasegawa's use of story is both empowering and arresting. In "The Crown Flower," a man ties dead monarch butterflies to nails and tacks them to his tangerine tree. When his wife dies, "a thick swarm of monarchs / covered every window of the house / pouring darkness / into everything." What I admire most about Hasegawa's poems is how she uses darkness to reveal what the world today desperately needs—the presence of light.

— Lisa Linn Kanae, author of *Sista Tongue*
and the short story collection *Islands Linked by Ocean*

La Chica's
Field Guide to
Banzai Living

La Chica's Field Guide to Banzai Living

Jennifer Hasegawa

OMNIDAWN PUBLISHING
OAKLAND, CALIFORNIA
2020

Cover art: Ken Price, *Levitating Sculpture*, 2006.
Acrylic, ink, and colored pencil on paper. 11 x 8.5 inches (28 x 22 cm).
© Ken Price, Inc. Courtesy Matthew Marks Gallery.

Cover typeface: Eurostyle LT Std, Avenir LT Std, & Bell Gothic LT Std
Interior typeface: Eurostyle LT Std & Adobe Garamond Pro

Cover design by Jennifer Hasegawa & Ken Keegan
Interior design by Ken Keegan

Offset printed in the United States
by Books International, Dulles, Virginia
On 55# Glatfelter B18 Antique
Acid Free Archival Quality Recycled Paper

Library of Congress Cataloging-in-Publication Data

Names: Hasegawa, Jennifer, 1970- author.
Title: La chica's field guide to banzai living / Jennifer Hasegawa.
Description: Oakland, California : Omnidawn Publishing, 2020.
Identifiers: LCCN 2019048432 | ISBN 9781632430786 (trade paperback)
Subjects: LCGFT: Poetry.
Classification: LCC PS3608.A78973 C48 2019 | DDC 811/.6--dc23
LC record available at https://lccn.loc.gov/2019048432

Published by Omnidawn Publishing, Oakland, California
www.omnidawn.com   (510) 237-5472   (800) 792-4957
10 9 8 7 6 5 4 3 2 1
ISBN: 978-1-63243-078-6

To Kikuo and Marilyn, who gave me life.

Propulsion Kingdom

Guidance Kingdom

Payload Kingdom

Propulsion Kingdom

Rockets with Rear-View Mirrors

They found a lack of
life on one of my planets,
despite the presence

of blood and water
in the soil. In space, as in
most things: *Go slow to*

go fast. They want to
colonize Mars because it
is the closest thing

they have to home. I
want more than an extra
39 minutes.

Venusian nights
last 100 days. Give me
the century to

comb through the sweet oil
of its atmosphere, survey
its lava fields, blind.

It's hot, but not hot
enough to melt our resolve
to fix it this time.

Propulsion units
burn out, disengage, and drop
to lower orbits.

Molten language
pollinates the voiceless to
birth the supernatural.

Astounding alien,
clean progenitor of the
new tongue of the ages.

She
is here.

21st Century Travel

We loaded the children
into capsules and shot them
into space.

They didn't have a chance
to learn their own names
before we had them holding
their stories in white plastic bags.

Featherless migrations
follow environmental triggers, too:

Days to live
grow shorter.

Fluctuating temperatures signal
mass graves nearby.

Water begins to flow
yellow.

In a tent
on the tip of a screw,
children eat
3 meals a day,
awaiting take-off.

They aren't hungry now,
but in a few years,
someone will need to teach them
how to smile.

Wash your face.
Eat this bread.

Do your best
to be credible:

Tell me
what you're afraid of
and maybe
we'll let you in.

☽

My bones
tell time.

My blood
drips pyramids.

Your fear
wants walls:

Tell me
what you're afraid of
and maybe
you'll find your way home.

To Anyone Who Can't Get Home

Including Natives, Immigrants, and Extraterrestrials

The false harbor of home:
washed ashore and alien
again.

> *This belongs to you.*
> *It does not belong to me.*

Before: the steamship
that delivered great-grand*X*.

Before: the brigantine
that brought coffee and the first Bible.

Before: the double-hulled canoe
that arrived to find it was not the first.

Slice the water:
the instinct to take up space.

Trace the trajectory:
the instinct to connect points.

From *Hawaiki,*
the place from which we came
and the place we will call home
when we die—back to Babylon,
where there was a tower built
by people speaking a common language.

From the urge to remember
and be remembered—
the *confundation* of language and meaning:
agents of the first
and eternal voyage away.

In darkness,
we pluck the gourd
from which we fling
pulp and seeds into light.

From the bloody mouth
and the destroyer,
we pluck
calamondin   thimbleberry   mountain apple
and delight
when we mistake the red fur of the tree fern
for a wild boar.

Every birth
is an act of colonization:
mongoose
born to mouse
born to grain.

In defense, we leave places
in exactness:
a typewriter on a desk,
chicken bones in a sink,
an empty bottle of perfume
on a nightstand.

But return
and return again
to these places
only to find ghosts
clicking keys,
touching bones,
and inhaling the last traces
of home.

Two-Minute Memoir

When I was 18,
I sold expensive clothes
at the mall.

Tourists and sex workers
were the only ones
who could ever afford
to buy anything.

Out on Kūhiō Avenue on a Friday night,
Chantal shouted:
    "*Hui!* Girlie! Like da dress? Looks good...right?"

> *And they were proud.*
> *And they saw that it was pleasing to the eye*
> *and that it was desired to make one wise.*

She set me up
to babysit
for the owner of the club
she danced at.

Tony had a baby
and an ex-wife with no septum.

As I stepped off the bus
at his house at midnight,
he'd get into a Rolls Royce
and drive to the club.

I'd put the baby to sleep
reading from my Astronomy
textbook: Mohorovičić discontinuity.

> *And the Lord God said,*
> *Behold,*
> *the man is become as one of us,*
> *to know good and evil.*

In the morning,
I'd heat the griddle
as the grill of his car
made its way through
the still-dark suburbs.

He'd pay me right
from a tight money clip
and eat a stack of hotcakes
like a sandwich.

> *And so they ate it*
> *and their eyes were opened.*

On his birthday night,
he put on his suit and python boots,
wandered around the house,
and passed out on his bed
with one leg hanging off the side.

> *And they made themselves*
> *garments of gold and lined them*
> *with the manes of lions.*

Those mice and their scissors!

And the lambs
with their switchblades
have cut the roars
out of the beasts.

Wake to a wavering
tower of tongues.

Hold the heavy paw
of time—its slowing pulse

tricking you into thinking
the future is farther, kinder
than it is.

Villanelle on Los Angeles 1992

She was half his size, but her arm was light years long.
He was straight-backed and strode in never-been-wet boat shoes.
How his soft honey hair jerked when Schoolgirl knocked him down.

Dookie braids escaped gravity on her head made strong
by the verdict of twelve strangers. No change of venue
as her fist to his face broadcast the news light years long.

Our heads bobbed against hazy bus windows all along
the route from Slauson to downtown, but as her fist flew
at McClintock, we all knew that Schoolgirl knocked him down.

The driver whistled low and switched his radio on
as the motor moaned to damns signaling corner coups
that would reveal a city, burn down blocks light years long.

Shopping carts rattled, careened unboxed TVs sidelong.
Out store doors flattened shoeboxes bloomed their grey pulp hues
while men on roofs held rifles 'cause Schoolgirl knocked him down.

Hair trigger, DUI, orange juice, and truncheon wrong
into law of brick and fire. Oh pyriscence, you cruise,
burn through resins, put a spit-shine on fear light years long.
Kam sa ham ni da. How you like us now? Schoolgirl knocked him down.

Carrying an M16 in the Garden of Eden

Alert in a corridor ▮▮▮ a ball rolled ▮▮▮▮ and I shot it. ▮▮▮
▮▮▮▮▮▮ patrolling ▮▮▮▮▮ at curfew ▮▮▮▮▮▮
▮ out of a corner ▮▮▮▮ he dropped ▮▮▮▮▮▮ like in ▮▮
practice. ▮▮▮▮▮ man ▮▮▮▮ behind a wall ▮▮▮▮▮
▮ blood ▮▮▮▮▮▮ like a twin ▮▮▮▮▮ I tucked myself into.
▮▮▮ his face ▮▮▮▮▮▮ taught me ▮▮▮▮▮
▮▮▮▮▮▮ I don't remember when ▮▮▮▮ I stopped ▮▮▮
▮▮▮▮ why don't I come ▮▮▮▮▮▮ or go ▮▮▮▮▮
Thanks dude, but ▮▮▮▮ I got to ▮▮▮▮▮ protect that hidden
▮▮▮▮▮▮ hole from which ▮▮▮▮▮ Fallujah ▮▮▮▮ ate
▮ until it was all gone ▮▮▮▮▮▮▮▮▮▮ fire ▮▮ dreams
and fire ▮▮▮▮ wake, they yelled ▮▮▮▮▮ 24/7 and I listened
▮▮ raining ▮▮▮▮ round after round, ▮▮▮▮ long range ▮▮
▮▮▮▮▮ and faceless ▮▮▮▮ in an office park ▮▮▮▮▮ ▮
▮▮▮▮▮▮ marrow ▮▮▮▮▮ gone.
▮▮▮ drink ▮▮▮▮▮ the last of the orange juice ▮▮▮▮▮
TV on all night ▮▮▮▮ every step ▮▮▮▮▮ wrong ▮▮▮▮
▮▮▮▮ and I long for ▮▮▮▮▮▮ my wings ▮▮▮▮
▮▮▮▮▮▮ trained ▮▮ to shoot ▮▮▮▮▮▮ not aim
▮ gassed ▮▮▮ with ▮▮ psychology ▮▮▮▮▮▮▮
▮▮▮▮ I ▮▮▮ signed those papers ▮▮▮▮ and now ▮▮▮▮
▮▮▮▮ the sun ▮▮▮▮▮▮▮▮▮▮▮ is homeless
▮▮▮▮▮▮ shadow in a doorway▮▮▮▮ as long as ▮▮▮▮
▮▮▮▮▮ the ▮▮▮▮▮▮▮ fingerprint ▮▮▮▮ of a bullet.

24

18 Minutes

What woke the birds that
morning, woke all. Shook too soon,
down sparked into flight.

Visibility
was good that day. It came in
low; tips see-sawed. Then,

it inverted and
everything went in. A vast
gray corpse bloomed from a

building. It was the
end of the long division
between skyscrapers

and planes. EngineDesk
WingChairCockpitPenNailSkin
Hair. It was not a

normal flight pattern.
My father motioned, *Come, look.*
The dull blue TV

light coated his face.
It took 18 minutes for
the words tumbling out

to turn from terror
to the -ism. That clean set
of seconds in which

u
    n
        i
           m
              a
                  g
                     i
                        n
                           a
                              b
                                 l
                                    e

precision looked like
a mistake. Watching so close,
we could not see the

second coming. What
dare fly in this air? The boom
flipped the room and bones

dropped from our pockets.
My father sucked his teeth and
mother demanded

we turn it off. She
was ready to take on the
day, not watch this torn,

bare body struggle
to right itself. *Don't watch, it's
disrespectful.* We

didn't look away
and now, somehow, all they want
us to do is watch.

This Love Like a Rock

My dad hauled home
a beautiful rock. It was three-feet tall
and pocked like a wild sponge.

When it rained, water pooled
in the top pocks and cascaded down
to fill the lower pocks.

He told my mom,
"*Pele* made em jus fo you, honey!"
She said, "Fairy tales."

The rock started making
its own water. I monitored it as it
slowly circled our house.

He ate some bad *opihi (auwe!)*
and was writhing in bed for days
as red moss crept across the rock.

Back at work, a boulder toppled
from the trench of a bulldozer
and caught his leg.

Earthbound meteor left a gash
in his shin. Blood pooled in the top pocks
and cascaded down to fill the lower pocks.

He hobbled out the front door,
gently tucked the rock into the bed of his truck
and we headed for Volcano town.

He returned it
to the grove of *ōhi'a lehua*
where he found it.

My father stared at his battered leg
and I worried that the rock would be
there waiting when we got home.

We listened to the urgent trill of the *ʻiʻwi,*
dipping its beak into the nectaries of the forest,
our pores wide open
                    and taking in
                                  our own sweet medicine.

The List of Retired Hurricane Names

At some point
you have to decide:
will you let folks
use your river
like a road?

Soon, the map of you
looks like a sweet loaf
cut up with a dull knife!

The levees of your body will tire
and you'll destroy the one
protecting Memory
to save the one
about to breach at Sleep.

On Charbonnet Street,
all of the women
can tell the story of the water;
of floating to the ceiling,
house dresses ballooning up to their ears
like jellyfish.

From the rooftops,
they called out
to swarms of swallows
tossed against the sky
like a plate of beans.

I climbed your levee
and people honked from their cars:

toaster oven   curtain rod   and a dead calf   on your banks.

According to the registry,
you're no longer free.
If you ran away,
they could arrest you
for stealing yourself.

Pantoum for Waiting

My father slips away in his rusty truck,
off to clear highways of cooled lava flows.
Dropped off before dawn, I'm greeted by a hot TV,
on all night talking to itself; no sleep for the electric.

Off to clear highways of cooled lava flows,
The Mom wakes first, smokes while she makes coffee.
The Stepdad appears in his underwear
and then quickly slides back into darkness.

The Mom wakes first, smokes while she makes coffee,
can't tell the difference between smoke and steam.
The Daughter pulls a curling iron through her hair.
She will grow up to be a beauty queen.

Can't tell the difference between smoke and steam.
Watching this family is like watching TV.
The Son's silver-capped tooth glints in the morning sun
as we pile into a primered VW bug.

Watching this family is like watching TV,
as we drive back to the house on the dead-end street.
The Daughter shows me her magic thumbtack.
She stores it on the bottom of her shoe.

This takes me back to the house on the dead-end street.
The Son says the magic hurts anyone who hurts us.
We're all so starving, we start to eat the house.
Drywall transforms into gingerbread before our eyes.

The Son says the magic hurts anything that hurts us.
The world is a witch and the oven stays shut
until there is nothing left but a thumbtack,
a silver tooth, and a hot quivering coal.

The world is a witch and the oven stays shut.
I see my father's truck approaching from darkness.
My mother has already left for the night shift.
The lady in the TV bathes, swaddles me in her pixelated arms.

The Hanuman Threshold

For Calculating Distances Without Physical Measure

Packs of lean girls lope
by. The gym teacher throws
his stopwatch at me.

I am walking around the track,
but in my mind, I am running:
running off the track
and up Kawili Street.

I pick up speed
down Komohana Avenue
with its rich-people houses
hidden behind monstera
and African tulip.

Up past Rainbow Falls,
I hear the ghosts of sovereignty
whistling for my attention.

I make the slow ascent
past the hospital
where we were all born
and where all of our mothers
will take their last good looks
up at our faces.

I run across the summit
of a dormant volcano,
and leap into the Pacific.
I am headed for India,
where I will hop trains
from Amritsar to Chennai.

On a train to Delhi,
with the doors wide open,
there is no difference
between inside
and outside.

I smell shit,
strawberries on the brink,
cut grass,
and dinners being made
in houses down the street
from everywhere.

I sway between two boys
picking at the ends of my scarf.
Their fingers invented touch
a million years ago,
but today they feel like newborn
hummingbirds.

I hold their hands in the temple
and as we pass through metal detectors
to enter the movie palace
where Aishwarya Rai will pump her shoulders
to conjure magic.

Bulldozer sifts through
a mound of garbage on the street;
unearths my missing heart
months after I've already left.

Hummingbird boys
grab it and run across traffic
miles deep. Crossing states,
they slow in Jaipur,
where they are showered
with curtains of lacquer bangles.

Heading south,
they take jobs as Mumbai dabbawallas,
delivering thousands of tiffins
without letter or number, and only color.

Pockets lined with cash,
they head to Goa,
where they gorge on fish curry rice
and collect bags of cashews
under the cover of night.

They hop on a barge
moving down River Mandovi,
carrying iron to seaworthy ships
at the Vasco de Gama docks,
ready for their journey
through the Arabian Sea
and on to Japan.

Docked in Kobe,
the boys shimmy into the lifeboats
of the *Taisei Maru,*
steadying itself
for its voyage to Hawai'i.

I see their oil-slicked heads of hair
bobbing in the distance.
Riding giant trevallies,
they raise my beating heart,
signaling like a buoy.

Guidance Kingdom

Marlon Brando's Master Class on Fate

I found a bone in
a storm of kelp. Knitted up
in the slimy green,

it smelled like a hot
night. I tucked it tight into
my palm and walked to

Marlon Brando's house.
He sat on his porch, wearing
his usual veil

of regret. He knew
immediately: finger
joint of a walking

whale. *Warm-blooded, like
you and me. They just found the
remains of one in*

*Pakistan. And you,
you found one on this atoll.*
What had my walking

whale held in its hands?
Lovers, leaves, mud, meat, sand, and
eventually

me. Marlon asked, *Where
will a feather dropped by a
seagull over the*

*heads of 2,000
men land?* You want it to be
random. But it ain't.

The International Order of Door-to-Door Salesmen

Out of work, I'd developed a rash
from being so stressed out
about being so broke.

I put on my faded red suit
and went to a mass interview at a Ramada Inn.
I found myself fighting for a chance
to sell funeral insurance,
door-to-door.

They gave me a stack of surveys.
Get the details:
What does she want her funeral to look like?
Get the signature:
We'll give you 70 bucks.

They gave me a binder of photos
of caskets,
of satin linings,
of flower arrangements.

They gave me a list
of names and addresses.

I visited homes,
like my parents' home:

Screen doors
fitted loosely into door jambs.

Wind chimes
shaped like owls and pagodas.

Porches swept
until brooms gave out.

Out of each door,
opened pensively,
if at all,
puffed the smell
of years of living,
of waiting.

One woman let me in
and talked me through photos
of her grandson
for two hours.

Another woman
made me a BLT
while I watched her son
shoot up on the sofa.

One man told me
to *fuck off and die.*
Address numbers nailed
to the front of his house
were painted on the bottoms
of empty sardine tins.

I stopped carrying the binder.
I put one survey on my clipboard
and just started walking
and knocking.

I arrived at a narrow Victorian
with its windows painted black.

A wall of a woman opened the door,
and smiled. Her eyes,
wrestling panda bears.

On one front tooth:
a gleaming gold cap with a star cutout.
On the other:
a crescent moon.

She regarded me and said:

> *You are as bare*
> *as the day you were born*
> *and that is beautiful,*
> *but you gotta get the hell*
> *off my porch.*

She passed her hand over my head
and a breeze moved down the block,
turning up leaves and balls of hair.

The unseen that gives and takes.
The instant magic of fear
and the slow-burrowing hoodoo
of suggestion.

Years later, there's a black chicken
threaded through the door handles
of a bank downtown. You step in the pool
of its blood and slip.

> *Damn,*
> *you're a hot thief in the night now*
> *with tons of cash*
> *and you put on at least 17 layers*
> *before you go anywhere.*

You hit the ground hard.
You are covered in blood.
All you see is flowers, all you feel
is satin.

The White Bull of Itaipu

Out of the *Gran Chaco,*
I ride with the dying doctor and his lover.
His blood is turning against him—
he is tired and in pain.

We pass fiery roadside stands of chickens
browning on spits, and slow only
for the cooing of dove-shaped breads
in *Doña Chinuka's* shop.

Township after township, we follow
an endless clothesline attended
to by bellbirds pinning up dresses
worn thin in the prettiest places.

Broom sellers wave us along.
Later, they will fall sleeping,
sweaty in their shacks, dreaming
their brooms into rifles.

We hear it, and then we are there: the dam
that wrestles a river to light a continent.
The doctor squeezes a weeping syringe
into his own arm. He tips into us

and then to the ground. His lover
takes the flower from her hair
and eats it.

Through the churning mist of the spillways,
I see him parading across tainter gates and concrete.

By a thin rope around his waist,
he leads a white bull,
bellowing for its master.

The Queen of Needles

For Philip Seymour Hoffman

This
is a do-over
for a master
of spinning
heavy cloaks.

Longing
for the armor of gods,
I dress
myself in chemicals
and the occult
of basketball.

I grace each day
with a half-boner
I call mastery
and a pet donkey
named fame.

You
who don't know who I am, but I bet you
couldn't do better. You
who eat up the beast like ice cream. Before you
know it, I'll
be on the short road
down the middle
age of morphine.

This
is, but I,
am not tragic!

I sing
to cheeseburgers!

I sing
to scotch!

I sing
to my children;
receding,
until all they get
is the moving
of my mouth.

Is it enough
to dispense of each day
in this way?

↓   *Tap the bar,*
        a slap on the face.

        Tap the bar,
        a punch in the gut.

        Tap the bar,
        a kick to the nuts.   ↑

Jack of spoons,
queen of needles:
make it go faster,
make me do
the things I hate most.

Drippy Leg Mystery Solved

I am a fourth edition product
of the United States.

I am loading...

I am a married divorced
actor singer dancer
known for my internet
reality TV show called "Reality"
about a real reality.

> *The state of things as they actually exist,*
> *rather than as they may appear or might be imagined.*

Hair by politics, make-up by business.

Entertainment gloss, tech foundation,
media mascara, and lifestyle shadow.

Culture top, comedy slacks,
healthy living belt, and local shoes.

> *In a wider definition, reality includes everything*
> *that is and has been,*
> *whether or not it is observable or comprehensible.*

Generally speaking, can you like me?
I have 76k and want to connect.

Featured posts holding up my fence include:

1. Trickle-Down Ugly
2. The Night I Got My First Bra Thrown Onstage
3. Heather Locklear: What Is She Running From?

> *A still more broad definition includes everything*
> *that has existed, exists, or will exist.*

Beyond my wall, stars
are stepping out,
including Betelgeuse
and Bellatrix.

Massive, luminous spheres
of plasma held together by gravity.

I love people who talk.
I tolerate question marks.
You admit to wasting
my time and $.
You act like you're the only one!

At the end of their lifetimes,
stars can also contain
a proportion of degenerate matter.

Though he died, they say he's
been made immortal
by French circus people.

A biological form able to live forever.

A forever in which
those who cannot remember the past
are condemned to eat it.

(F)laws

He glowed wonder when
he saw the ground giving them
up. Waxy skins peeled

back, revealing brown
gleaming in borderlands sun.
He thumped the globes for

answers; heard rustling
in low-hanging mesquite and
in the stillness in

between leaves lowed the
hearts' acknowledgment. For this,
he thanked, grasped, and plucked,

in a good way. So
happy he would have floated
off if the antler

palm hadn't snared his
shoelace and escorted him
back to his truck. At

checkpoint, uniforms
smashed every one with hammers,
looking for kilos

of cocaine growing
in gourds. Flaws in the mind are
replicated on

the land. Skins cracked, seeds
shivering. Flaws in the mind
are replicated

on the body. Guard
said *Stop your crying. It's just
gourds.* He said *These are*

the hearts of the deer.
Bodies poised and muscular,
listen for them come

for you in the night.
Metal totem whirring with
the flawed focusing

of glass eyes upon
you *so accustomed to the
sound of surveillance*

you suspect it is
the tune of existence.
Thump. Thump. Thump. This is

the sound of velvet
grazing against fresh concrete.
2,000 miles, bleeding.

The Ancient History of David Bowie

When my cousin Dean was sixteen,
he had his psychotic break.

He believed he had to pick up David Bowie
from the airport.

I wanted to believe him.
I wanted to go with him.
I watched my uncle wrestle him
to the floor.

Dean would've driven David
and me down Banyan Drive,
like all the older kids do
on a Sunday afternoon –
>blasting Cecilio & Kapono
>mascara
>tight jeans
>pocket comb
>feathered hair
>gold chain
>*pakalōlō*
>cherry lip gloss.

We'd check David in
to the Hukilau Hotel
where Dean's mom cleans rooms
and spends evenings
in the laundry room with Kimo,
who is missing an eye,
but says that the remaining one
is sweet on her.

We'd take David downtown
where the *mahu*
brave-wigged, strong-legged, and lipsticked
stand sentry to the alley
between the barbershop
and the movie theater.

If a family has five sons, the sixth may be raised as a daughter to do the work of women.
And so his mother said, you, the sixth, the boy closest my corpse, will be the next noble woman.
Sequential hermaphrodite, *mahu, aikāne:* The bridge back to the garden.

Her brother lay with the king, as lover and counselor, chanter and spokesman—*aikāne.*
She saw the people with golden books arrive and the infinite sexes became two.
If a family has five sons, the sixth may be raised as a daughter to do the work of women.

These days, she sleeps in salt water. Nights, she cruises the street between the barbershop
and the movie theater. Tonight, she swears she saw David Bowie.
If a family has five sons, the sixth may be raised as a daughter to do the work of women.
Sequential hermaphrodite, *mahu, aikāne:* The bridge back to the garden.

My dad went to that barbershop
for 50 years, until his barber died.
Toward the end,
he'd come home with lopsided cuts:

"Dat buggah goin' blind!"
my dad mock-complained,
as he looked into a mirror
and ran a comb down
the side of his head.

Dean and I went to that movie theater
whenever my mom could spare a few dollars.

The movies were rarely
more interesting than the fireflies
hovering in damp corners.

They danced amongst dust,
illuminating their partners
with ferocity
and sly vengeance.

When All You Have is Good Intentions and a Toilet Brush

Walter gathered them by flashlight
from the edges of the festering pond
behind his house.

    Bufo Marinus. Cane toad. Their pupils are horizontal. Their irises, golden.

When Walter talked back,
his father would take a freshly cut chili pepper
and rub it across his gums.

        Glands behind their ears seep a poison.

Walter's mother wore
shiny nylon nightgowns
while driving around town
in a cherry red van.

    Absorbed through the eyes, the poison may cause pain and temporary blindness.

My mom told Walter
to stay away from our house
and so,
in the release of night,
he slapped his bare feet
over to our driveway,
where he tipped a bucket
and ran.

        The male mating call sounds like a distant motorboat.

When we drove up,
our headlights fell upon an army.

My mom walked slowly through the field
of bumpy backs and low leaping.

Once inside, she shook an entire can of cleanser
into the bathtub.

The toilet brush in her hand poked at the air,
like a torch, like a sword.

Surface Tension

(or You Can't Free Yourself If You Don't Know You're Locked Up)

There's a ring in town
Trina wants to buy
so she says she's gonna
stop at the casino
to get some cash.

      Systems of tension buy us things.

She speeds across
the casino floor, taps buttons
and swipes hot hands
across screens like a magician.

      Systems of tension make us move.

She throws herself
into the bonus round
as if she has only known
winning.

      Systems of tension are fed by fingers
      crossed tightly in pockets.

Deafening light,
blinding touch—

in utero casino

—tracing
latitudes of wealth,
longitudes
of
power.

I remember a time
when the only thing
I hadn't lost
was my body.
And so I said to myself:
Sell it then!

Call it corporeal entrepreneurship
backed by
algorithms,
rainbows of pills,
and 20 ounces of road
rage in a speeding car
with no driver.

Robots will keep
the surface taut,
until they can not.

And when it breaks,
they'll call it an apocalypse,
but our hands
will be unbound.
And our faces,

oh our glistening faces

will flex in recognition;
flash their alphabet of atoms,
to spell out a new world
of glorious rocks
and fascinating residues.

More Than a White Mountain

We'd never looked more
unlike ourselves. Small heathens,
building a snowman

in the belly button
of a god. My mom is wearing
a knit cap with a

vigorous pom-pom
and a sweater that makes her
look like she's covered

in popcorn. I'm in
a turtleneck and mittens.
I'm wearing mittens!

My dad looks most like
himself, wearing his same old
windbreaker, the color

of deli mustard,
because not even freezing
temperatures will

make him admit that
nature's nature is stronger
than his own. We have

our hands deep in snow.
This is the last time my mom
will smile out of joy.

From here on out, smiles
are born of relief. Dad looks
triumphant, his gaze

surveying the stark
landscape as if it were the
surface of the moon.

Our snowman has rocks
for a face and looks more like
a giant mound of

grated daikon than
a stack of three styrofoam
balls, like on TV.

Our technique is off,
but I've never felt better,
finally doing

something that I've seen
only white people doing.
The sun is sliding

down the face of the
sky father and my mom says
she's getting too cold.

We shovel some snow
into the bed of my dad's
truck as if to say,

this time will not melt.
Drive down the mountain, past the
military camp,

barren lands claw
into forest. *Palila,*
honeycreeper, sings

out colonizers.
Alien starts to wear off
or return. Back in

mango land, the hot
pavement cooks up surplus sweet
bodies, bursting skins

open. Mom pulls off
her knit cap. Dad unzips his
windbreaker and tugs

at the ribbed collar
of his white t-shirt, calling
back the sanity

of sea-level life.
Look at my mittened hands. What's
the thrill of being

unable to grasp
anything? *Maunakea*
now spread tall in the

distance. The snow we
dug our hands into. White cape
draped over muscled

shoulders of creation. Roll
down window. Peel off soggy
mittens. Toss them out

the window; the first,
and certainly not the last,
concession.

Payload Kingdom

Kamikazes à Paris

Tunisian sisters
lived in a quaint flat downtown
then, they moved into

a handful of dust. Have you
been to Paris? What was it like?

O

Ghosts sell stale bread in
the market. It will be a
while until even

the Mother of Satan shows
her gleaming face there again.

O

The girl knew it was
time to go, but kept dancing
toward a home always

just another mile away.
Liberty legs took her there.

O

If they were allowed
to carry, it would have been
a much, much different

situation. Carry it
now: baby, book, water, head.

◑

They found a finger.
They found the brother and showed
it to him and asked

Did you loosen it, sever
it from the body now too

vast and multitudinous
to be placed into a bag?

◑

An explosion is
the product of disorder.
Unmasked, confident:

Choose your seeds with intention—
sow 3, 4 times, then reload.

Gen Z

When she was born, they
buried her mother, roasted
her like a wild pig.

Wrapped her in big leaves
placed hot stones against her flesh.
It was not cruel

at the time. The child
was raised by a dog, instead.
They roved through forests,

tracking wild bucks and
honing communication
without words. She licked

blood off his whiskers,
triggering the scent that says
resilience. They

lay in each other's
arms in the late afternoon,
sun scattered across

their bodies like a
rash. In what we would call an
envisioning, but

which a dog just calls
seeing, the child turns blue in
mood. The dog knows that

it is just about
saving enough breath to blow
through the bad endings.

Black hibiscus sings
to the dog, tells him that to
turn on the furnace,

twist the dials in the
medulla oblongata.
You want to cremate

bodies of envy,
evaporate self-loathing.
The child's teeth are in

rows, like a choir.
This is reassuring to
the dog, as they walk

through each doorway in
the village, the dog barking
its approval as

the child howls out doubt,
wide-mouthed and turning all
circumstances, inside out.

The Slow Decay of Mystery

Uncle Kaz wore combat fatigues
to mow his lawn
and woke his basset hound each morning
by prodding her with a length of rubber hose.

When the winter floods came,
Uncle Kaz's house
at the bottom of the hill
got it the worst.

His garage became a swimming pool
and all of us kids would stand
at its edge, dreaming
of back- and butterfly strokes.

The neighborhood men
would stand knee-deep
in water, staring into the mouth
of the overflowing gully.

Their wives' cheeks blushed
through living room windows
watching their husbands, macho
and puffed up by the elements.

But these guys
were just talking
about whether the rain
would stop
in time for the cockfight.

They kept the world
wild and left
the problem solving
to chance.

Uncle Kaz's daughter Tita
had sad eyes like his dog.
She left school
midway through pre-algebra.

By the time I saw her again,
I was failing phys ed
and she was pushing a stroller
past the gully.

I called to her, but her walk
had no more room for stories
about boys born in peaches
and fireballs chasing men
through cane fields.

I lay in bed that night, watching
termites crowd the window screen.
And then, as if it had never happened before,
the geckos strolled in and ate every single one.

The giant hand
under my bed
said to the shadow
that held me
down in the night:

Don't let her figure you out!
Without us,
who knows
what she'll do.

The Crown Flower

Our neighbor collected the dead
monarchs, still and scattered
beneath the branches of his beloved
crown flower bush.

He'd gently tie their bodies
to heavy iron nails
and dangle them
from his tangerine tree.

After his wife died,
he found 100 tiny
empty whiskey bottles
in the drawers of her sewing table.

After finishing a bottle,
she'd pluck one of his beauties
fluttering in the wind, and use it
to dab the liquor from her lips.

When she took her last breath,
a thick swarm of monarchs
covered every window of the house,
pouring darkness
into everything.

Alien Life Forms

When nothing cute fills it, these other things do:
close bundles of blood, water, and interstellar gases.

Consider, perhaps the egg is afraid?
So, I keep it on a short leash

orbiting an ovary; tiny astronaut
out on a space walk. In no time,

there are a multitude torquing around.
Space is unlimited. Soon, my uterus is 10-feet tall.

I have never been more female!
My uterine universe shines brighter

than science thought it could. I carry a full life
of lives everywhere I go. This one is a lawyer,

this one a moody poet, and yet another,
a prima ballerina in an endometrial tutu.

But mama's tired and it's time
to leave this cave. I radio out

to my pulsing web of unconceived
children: Be good. Remember, I've loved you.

Control snips the cables and I watch
them float away. Dissolving into dark matter,

they're giggling or crying. I can't really tell,
but let's say, please, giggling.

A Black Hole Operator Speaks

Yes, there had been salmonella,
but this dining room was my place to write.

Sure, it was fast food that resembled nothing
of its declared origins, but what ever does?

A family of eight communed
over trays of colas and chalupas.

Lola, arms spread across her corner booth,
fired commands in Tagalog into her headset.

They understood the beauty of this place
that had united the taco and the fried chicken.

The Colonel stared out of a frame on the wall. All at once,
he looked White, Black, Chicano, Asian, and Everything

better
together.

Brown lumps under heat lamps, is it chicken?
Corn? Wood? On my tray, is it taco? Pie? Purse?

I got a token for the bathroom. A fly
occupied the space with me.

I flushed and felt something on the handle.
I blasted my hand with hot water. I pumped soap.

I had another human's shit on my finger
and I started to hallucinate.

Toxic Shock appeared as a white stallion
stomping its front hoof, imploring me to jump on.

Dysentery was Madonna wanting, needing,
waiting for me to justify her love.

Then Hep C showed up and took me back
to the afternoon in a remote bathroom at work

      where I found a woman at a sink
      washing her hands; her hands

      encased in thick clouds
      of suds, like boxing gloves.

      She was young with red hair
      and a long string of pearls.

      She didn't look up. She didn't stop.
      She was washing for the end,

      widening that gap between herself
      and the final processing

      of what cannot be absolved,
      of what cannot be absorbed.

Back at my table, my finger bloated and red,
the ringing in my ears shook the crumbs across the mesa.

Eighty degrees with a dusting of wheat, dander, water,
cellulose, and light. Tiny world rose up all around me,

microbes and their fine net that ensnares all.
The universal program to feed, reproduce, and die

until we meander too close to that magnificent keeper
where all things end, again and again.

Orbiting the rim of bent light: the family of eight,
your Lola, the Colonel, a clutch of hens, and an infinity

of your selves, slowing, reddening, and finally
spaghettified through the cosmic sphincter

tightened by gravity herself. Finally witness
and subject to the alchemic singularity!

The operator chuckles and shakes its head:
You dumb fucks've been wasting your time

keeping them separate. Purity. Filth.
It's all the same here.

The Surveyors

Her father paved roads.
He'd bring her road reflectors
to use as paper
weights. They looked bigger
on her desk
than they did on the road.

During storms, he'd drive
her through parking lots,
pointing out
how he'd molded asphalt
to channel rushing water
straight into storm drains.

                    tripod
                theodolite
                  compass
                    level

On such a rainy day,
her car slipped
across the line
and hung
by its rear axle
from a bridge.

Eyes on the waves below,
she watched the birds
perched along the pylons,
black with white-ringed necks.

They spread their wings,
demanded space,
and dove
into the foaming bay.

The Orinda Diamond Mine

I can't tell you that
this will be the last time you'll
have to pick me up,

cold and naked, in
front of a gas station down
the street from the house

where I was born a
debutante astronaut. Cops
coax slow fog into

the canyon bowl and
scan the horizon for the
flash of your headlights.

Again, I've landed
on a planet where I know
all food will kill me.

It is not about
placing a mass in my mouth.
It is about *4*.

F	O	O	D
1	2	3	4

If I eat what you
offer, I'll need to eat 3
more. In the market,

I heard a growl from
a large dog I could not find.
Then, I heard your voice

as I bent over
to put on my underwear:
Fat. You drive up in

your red sports car and
lecture me on how they'll
find intelligent

life one day while I
sit bare-assed on a speed bump.
You, the patrician,

the charismatic
macrofauna, exact the
lingo of labs on

feeling. I unfurl
a thousand reels of my most
intimate thoughts—and

I'm still a stranger
to myself. *My mind is a
diamond. Clever gem
cutter, set me free.*

Knife Shopping

Every winter,
my father goes
knife shopping.

The store is a hallway
slipped between
the scent of tractor tires
and steam-cleaned manure.

Knives are strapped
to walls of velvet, steel,
or wood—hinting
at what their blades
are meant to cleave.

Sleek limbs
of ritual and work
rattle for his attention.

He flips open his
pocket knife, runs it undernose
to inhale ghost of tree, fruit, and fish,
and walks out.

Back home,
he wets his sharpening stone
and pulls his old blade
a 1,000 times through
the grey slurry of self-control.

Telekinetic Lullaby

When I was little, the kind woman next door
died.

I asked my mom what cancer
is and she said, *It's extra tissue in your body.*

Oh the hours spent imagining
my body as a box of tissues, overflowing.

I watched her husband in their garden,
snipping limp azalea branches and adjusting rocks.

At bedtime, I peered out my window
overlooking their house. It was dark and still,

until he started playing the harmonica.
By the time he got to the opening bars

of *The Yellow Rose of Texas,* his windows
glowed gold and I could see him

sitting on their bedroom floor,
hands wrapped around his harmonica, mind focused

on stilling all of those troublesome rocks
that insist on moving
on their own volition.

Ode to Pepeʻekeo Mill Camp

Grandma's house is held
together by a dozen rusty nails
and inhabited
by colonies of wild cane.

The front door
is covered in lichen,
growing in patterns
that type out essays
on forgetting.

The road to her house
crumbles at the edges
and is split down the center.

I scan the land
for a shred of aloha
fabric from grandma's rag mop
or a shard of the tin roof
that banged out bossa novas
in rain storms.

In the sting
of cane arrow
against heart,
I see her stepping
into the raging overgrowth,
her gray polyester dress
hiked above her wrinkled knees.

Moving farther into the breach,
deeper into the gulch of time,
where will she emerge?

After The Islands, c. 1961

For Agnes Martin

I am a wavering cloth.
I am a field of snow.
I am an infinite braid.
I am a traffic jam.
I am a spinal cord.
I am a hand-knitted sweater.
I am a crumpled sheet of paper.
I am a bowl of popcorn.
I am a fingernail collection.
I am a good person.
I am a good.
I am a person.
I am drawn
by every hand.

Prayer Ceramic

For Ken Price

Start

It was the perfect dumpster,
sparking like a roadster,
and spitting the kind of stink
and juicy trash required
to construct the future.

Got a million dollars, walk down
Figueroa at 4 am, 39 cent taco
here
and leg of gree-see chicken
there.

Spend the morning
in an immaculate bathroom,
unwanted obsessions
tracing veins between
each excruciating cramp,

pushing toxic organica
from mouth and sphincter
through elaborate tunnels
paved with gold
and gingered salmonella rods.

Before

As for construction of the past,
the white noise
in which *Homo sapiens* love
with superaction and slap
each other's faces so hard

every pair of sunglasses
ever owned fly
off into the street
like a flock of sick birds:
what of it?

Now

Run to river, mountain, valley, shore;
trout, eagle, grizzly, bee.
Gawk with awe and then shoot
at close range. Bang
ruffles stiff science across the scape.

This
is a feast of human sperm
and horse ova! The offal of rich
data melts on contact. Stuffed
with conflict and never felt better.

When

Out on the terrace of lights,
warm interplanetary winds
lift my hair and turn it
into time itself.
Tick-tock.

Spin a lump.
Susurrus of the wheel
between thighs
sings flippity-flap
lubed with slip.

Raise walls!
Dam glossy broth
of youth to stop
the sloppy oatmeal
of age.

Shouting prayers at greenware,
davening that you might
not crack. Baby, I picked
you up and lifted you
into the fire.

End

The world is alarmed
at two feet.

(The world is alarmed
at two feet.)

The flat-foot of death came,
but so did fame.

Most of the time,
it starts with a teapot,
but on rare occasions,
it ends
with a universe.

Notes

Two-Minute Memoir: Includes riffs on Genesis 3:6, 3:7, 3:21, and 3:22.

Villanelle on Los Angeles 1992: This poem begins with a scene I witnessed on the afternoon of April 29, 1992. It documents the moment at which everyone on a bus I was on understood that a not-guilty verdict had been delivered in the trial against four Los Angeles Police Department officers accused of beating Rodney King. The beating had been filmed and broadcast widely to the public. The footage showed officers striking King with their batons 56 times.

The verdict was delivered at 3:15 p.m. By 5 p.m., rioting across Los Angeles had begun. Businesses were looted and buildings burned. More than 50 people were killed and over 2,000 people were injured. By the time rioting slowed six days later, 13,500 troops, including the National Guard, Marines, and federal police, had been deployed throughout the city.

Carrying an M16 in the Garden of Eden: This poem is rooted in my reading of *Soul Repair: Recovering from Moral Injury after War* by Rita Nakashima Brock and Gabriella Lettini. The book quotes Kevin Benderman, U.S. Army combat veteran, in *Soldiers of Conscience*:

> *[I found out] we were in the area of Iraq that was supposed to be the Garden of Eden, the cradle of civilization where mankind began. I had to ask myself, "Why am I carrying around an M16 in the Garden of Eden?"*

18 Minutes: The title of this poem is rooted in my watching of New York City local TV news coverage of the September 11 attacks available on YouTube.

The List of Retired Hurricane Names: Hurricanes are named in alphabetical order according to a static list that restarts every six years. Each year, the World Meteorological Organization accepts requests from countries to retire the names of particularly destructive hurricanes and replaces the names with other names. For example, Katrina was retired from the list and replaced by Katia. The name is removed for at least 10 years to avoid confusion and the resurfacing of memories of the destruction caused by the storm.

Marlon Brando's Master Class on Fate: This poem is rooted in the following statement from Marlon Brando, published in the *Los Angeles Times* on May 23, 1990: "The messenger of misery has come to my house, and has also come to the house of Mr. Jack Drollet in Tahiti."

(F)laws: In January 2019, the Tohono O'odham Nation convened a human rights hearing for the United Nations Expert Mechanism on the Rights of Indigenous Peoples in the context of borders, migration, and displacement. This poem is rooted in testimony I witnessed at this hearing.

The Ancient History of David Bowie: The poem embedded in this poem is rooted in my reading of portions of the following texts:

Robertson, C. (1989). The Māhū of Hawaiʻi. *Feminist Studies* 15, 313-326.

Wallace, Lee (2003). *Sexual Encounters: Pacific Texts, Modern Sexualities.* Ithaca, NY: Cornell University Press.

Kamikazes à Paris: This poem is rooted in my watching of news coverage of the November 2015 Attacks on Paris. I heard the voices of Parisian witnesses softly repeat "*Kamikaze... Kamikaze... Kamikaze...*" in French, as the English translation repeated loudly over it: "Suicide bomber... Suicide bomber... Suicide bomber..."

Ode to Pepeʻekeo Mill Camp: My paternal grandmother and I did not speak the same language, but we played raucous hands of *hanafuda*. She often just sat and watched me as if I were a beautiful alien. She cooked *sekihan* for me. She snuck me single dollar bills and *ume* candies when my parents weren't looking. I believe she died of a broken heart. She's never left me. It feels like she could step into my living room at any moment.

Prayer Ceramic: This poem is rooted in my learning of the passing of Ken Price, an American artist who made ceramic sculpture. He was also my art ceramics professor. We may have shared 100 words in total, but his silent nods opened up a safe space for me to test the physics of clay and language. Ken Price's drawing, *Levitating Sculpture*, appears on the cover of this book.

Acknowledgements

Thank you to Truong Tran, without whom this book would not exist. His decades of support kept me writing, kept me living. It is because of his selfless championing of fellow creators that the world knows the words of so many writers, like myself, who might have otherwise been overlooked.

Thank you to Rusty Morrison, Ken Keegan, Kayla Ellenbecker, and Omnidawn for reading my work with open hearts and for sharing their energy and expertise with me to manifest this book.

Thank you to the people associated with the following publications where versions of some of these poems first appeared: *The Adroit Journal, Bamboo Ridge, Standing Strong: Japantown and Fillmore,* and *Tule Review*.

Thank you to the San Francisco Foundation and the Joseph Henry Jackson Award for supporting the development of this book.

Thank you to Kikuo Hasegawa and Marilyn Hasegawa (née Sakai) for their love. By reading to me as a child, my parents taught me how to imagine worlds beyond the one in front of me. With that, they made anything possible.

Thank you to Dennis J Bernstein for his perfect love of this imperfect human, for naming me a poet when I wavered in belief, and for writing in solidarity. He brings joy, feeling, and focus to my life, which made writing this book possible.

Thank you to Quarry Pak for her friendship, curiosity, and singular genius.

Thank you to Ken Price for his art and the integrity of his teaching practice, both of which inform my poetry to this day. **Thank you** to the family of Ken Price and the Matthew Marks Gallery for allowing me to use Ken Price's drawing, *Levitating Sculpture*, on the cover of this book.

Thank you to Women Who Submit-San Francisco for helping me to believe in my work. Keep the bell ringing.

Thank you to Shizue Seigel for bringing the power of writing to the people.

Thank you, BELIEF. The difference between writing a poem and not writing a poem is the belief that, once written, the poem has a purpose in the world. To anyone reading this and wondering, "Should I keep writing? Who cares?" If you care, I care.

Illuminate the world with your words. Without them, we are condemned to live by only the fading light of what already exists.

La Chica's Field Guide to Banzai Living
by Jennifer Hasegawa

Cover art: Ken Price, *Levitating Sculpture,* 2006.
Acrylic, ink, and colored pencil on paper. 11 x 8.5 inches (28 x 22 cm).
© Ken Price, Inc. Courtesy Matthew Marks Gallery.

Cover typeface: Eurostyle LT Std, Avenir LT Std, & Bell Gothic LT Std
Interior typeface: Eurostyle LT Std & Adobe Garamond Pro

Cover design by Jennifer Hasegawa & Ken Keegan
Interior design by Ken Keegan

Printed in the United States
by Books International, Dulles, Virginia
On 55# Glatfelter B19 Antique
Acid Free Archival Quality Recycled Paper

Publication of this book was made possible in part by gifts from
Katherine & John Gravendyk in honor of Hillary Gravendyk,
Francesca Bell, Mary Mackey, and The New Place Fund

Omnidawn Publishing
Oakland, California
Staff and Volunteers, Spring 2020

Rusty Morrison & Ken Keegan, senior editors & co-publishers
Kayla Ellenbecker, production editor
Gillian Olivia Blythe Hamel, senior editor & book designer
Trisha Peck, senior editor & book designer
Rob Hendricks, marketing assistant & *Omniverse* editor
Cassandra Smith, poetry editor & book designer
Sharon Zetter, poetry editor & book designer
Liza Flum, poetry editor
Matthew Bowie, poetry editor
Juliana Paslay, fiction editor
Gail Aronson, fiction editor
Izabella Santana, fiction editor & marketing assistant
SD Sumner, copyeditor